Egg Recipes for Beginners

Super Easy-to-Prepare Meals Especially for Those New to the Experience of Cooking

BY - Alain Duke

Copyright Notification

Table of Contents

Introduction

Egg-Based recipes are not only suitable to eat for breakfast, but they can be eaten at any time of the day! My collection of egg-based recipes include a wide array of yummy dishes that you will choose to serve for lunch and dinner meals. Maybe you have decided to cut back on the amount of meat that is included in your diet. Whatever your reasons, you can feel good knowing that eggs like meat are a great source of protein. The recipes that I have included are all simple and easy-to-prepare. You can quickly whip up a good protein-filled recipe from this collection that will leave you feeling satisfied.

These recipes vary in cook time from 5 minutes to 55 minutes, fairly quick all under an hour in cook time. You will soon learn how to prepare great dishes with eggs from breakfast, lunch, dinner and even dessert recipes! It is now time for you to begin cooking your egg-based meal by following one of these recipes—happy cooking!

Collection of Healthy Egg-Based Recipes

1. Egg Bourek

Enjoy this tasty and easy-to-prepare egg-based treat with your loved ones!

Prep time: 15 minutes

Cook time: 30 minutes

Servings: 8

Ingredients:

- 3 eggs
- 6 sheets Filo pastry
- ½ teaspoon Bicarbonate soda
- ½ cup butter, melted
- ¼ cup milk
- 1 cup feta cheese, chopped
- 1 cup Greek yogurt
- 1 egg
- ½ cup grated cheddar cheese
- 1/3 cup sparkling water
- extra 2 tablespoons of grated cheddar for topping

Directions:

Set your oven to 400° Fahrenheit and grease the casserole dish with some butter.

Whisk 3 eggs, yogurt, milk and sodium bicarbonate together in a bowl. Add the feta cheese and ½ cup of grated cheddar cheese.

In another bowl, whisk the sparkling water and 1 egg together.

Arrange one sheet of filo on the bottom of the prepared casserole dish. Spread some of the cheese mixes on top of the sheet.

Place another sheet of filo on top, then soak it with the egg/water mixture. Repeat this process until you have used up all the filo and cheese fillings.

Top with extra 2 tablespoons of grated cheddar cheese and bake for 30 minutes. Remove from your oven and allow to cool for a few minutes before slicing. Serve and enjoy!

2. Sweetcorn & Pea Fritters

This is a tasty recipe for fritter lovers that is sure to please!

Prep time: 10 minutes

Cook time: 6 minutes

Servings: 8

Ingredients:

- 1 tablespoon olive oil
- 1 teaspoon baking powder
- 3 eggs
- ½ cup flour
- ½ cup sweet corn
- 3 green onions, finely chopped
- ½ cup frozen peas, defrosted
- 1 cup Cottage cheese
- ½ cup milk

Directions:

Begin by whisking the eggs, cheese, flour, milk and baking powder together. Stir in the peas, sweetcorn and onions.

In a large frying pan, heat oil over medium heat. Add fritter shapes to a heated pan and cook for about 3 minutes per side. Repeat until the batter has been used and serve immediately and enjoy!

3. Spanish Popovers

Enjoy this yummy egg-based dish as a light lunch or breakfast meal!

Prep time: 10

Cook time: 25 minutes

Servings: 2

Ingredients:

- 2 eggs
- 2 tablespoons olive oil
- ¾ cup milk
- ½ cup water
- ½ cup pepperoni, sliced
- 1 ¾ cups flour

Directions:

Preheat your oven to 400° Fahrenheit and add oil to a 12-serving muffin tin.

Whisk all ingredients in a large mixing bowl, then leave them to rest overnight in the fridge.

Place the prepared muffin tin into the oven and heat for about 5 minutes.

Remove the tray and add the mixture to the muffin tray evenly. Bake for about 25 minutes or until they are puffed up and golden brown in colour.

Serve and enjoy immediately!

4. Egg & Bagel

It makes for the perfect tasty breakfast or lunch meal!

Prep time: 5 minutes

Cook time: 10 minutes

Servings: 1

Ingredients:

- 1 Gherkin pickle sliced
- 1 egg
- 1 bagel
- ½ red onion, finely diced
- 1 beef tomato, sliced
- 1 teaspoon olive oil
- 1 Portobello mushroom, sliced
- ½ teaspoon yellow mustard
- 1 tablespoon tomato sauce
- 1 slice of cheese

Directions:

In a frying pan, over medium heat, warm the oil. Add the egg and cook for a few minutes.

Add the mushroom and red onion and continue to cook and stir to combine. Once cooked, remove from heat and keep warm.

Toast the bagel, then place the bottom on a plate. Spread the mustard and tomato sauce, then top with mushrooms and onions. Add the fresh tomato slices and egg and cheese. Top with the other half of the bagel. Serve with a pickle on the side, and enjoy!

5. Egg Breakfast Muffins

This is a wonderful and healthy egg-based recipe perfect for breakfast time!

Prep time: 8 minutes

Cook time: 20 minutes

Servings: 12

Ingredients:

- 5 eggs
- 1 teaspoon sea salt (fine)
- 2 cups milk
- 3 tablespoons pine nuts
- ½ cup cottage cheese
- 1 tablespoon chives, chopped
- ¼ cup tomatoes, chopped
- ½ cup bacon pieces, finely chopped
- garnish with chopped tomatoes & torn basil leafs

Directions:

Preheat the oven to 400° Fahrenheit and grease the 12-hole muffin tin with some butter.

Whisk milk, salt and eggs together in a mixing bowl.

Add the cheese and chopped chives to the egg mixture. Divide the mixture evenly among holes in the muffin tray. Sprinkle chopped tomatoes and bacon on top.

Bake for 20 minutes or until puffed up and golden in colour. Allow cooling for a few minutes, then serve with fresh tomatoes and basil leafs on top and enjoy!

6. Eggs in Avocado

A tasty dish that is also very pleasing to the eye; give it a try!

Prep time: 8 minutes

Cook time: 8 minutes

Servings: 2

Ingredients:

- 2 eggs
- 1 tablespoon freshly grated Parmesan cheese
- 1 Avocado
- 1 tablespoon pumpkin seeds
- 1 tablespoon sunflower seeds

Directions:

Preheat your oven to 400° Fahrenheit. Line a baking tray with parchment paper.

Cut the avocado in half and remove the stone. Place each half with the skin side facing down on the prepared baking tray.

Crack an egg into each hole in the avocado. Sprinkle with seeds and cheese, then bake for about 8 minutes. Serve immediately and enjoy!

7. Creme Brulee

Enjoy this lovely light and dreamy sweet, tasting egg-based treat!

Prep time: 10 minutes

Cook time: 45 minutes

Servings: 4

Ingredients:

- 4 egg yolks
- ¼ cup sugar (plus 2 tablespoons extra)
- 1 1/3 cups cream
- 1 teaspoon vanilla extract

Directions:

Begin by preheating your oven to 300° Fahrenheit—grease four ramekins with butter. Boil a kettle of water and get a casserole dish out.

Mix the cream, egg yolks, vanilla and sugar in a bowl.

Pour the egg mixture evenly between the ramekins, then place them inside the casserole dish. Pour enough boiling water into a casserole dish to come up halfway up the ramekins.

Place into the oven and bake for about 45 minutes or until the top looks a little crusty.

Remove ramekins from the casserole dish and allow them to cool at room temperature.

Sprinkle extra sugar over top and using a chef's torch or high grill setting, caramelize the tops of brulees. Serve with fresh fruit if you like, and enjoy!

8. Portuguese Tarts

This a yummy recipe that tart lovers are sure to enjoy!

Prep time: 5 minutes

Cook time: 25 minutes

Servings: 24

Ingredients:

- 4 egg yolks
- 1 sheet puff pastry
- 2 eggs
- 2 cups sugar
- 3 teaspoons lemon zest
- 1 cinnamon stick
- ¾ cup milk
- ¼ cup cornstarch
- 1 teaspoon vanilla extract
- powdered sugar and ground cinnamon for garnish

Directions:

Preheat the oven to 425° Fahrenheit and grease a 12-hole muffin tin with butter.

Roll out the pastry so it is a long rectangular shape, then roll it up a long way to create a sausage shape. Slice into 24 disks.

Roll each disk to create a flat circle and add it to the bottom of the muffin holes.

Bring the sugar and half a cup of water to a boil to create a sugar syrup. Add the cinnamon stick and lemon zest to the sugar syrup. Boil and stir until thick, then remove the cinnamon stick and lemon. Leave the syrup to cool.

Whisk the eggs and cornstarch together in a bowl. Heat your milk and vanilla extract in a pan over medium heat. Slowly add in the eggs and whisk and cook. Add the sugar syrup and mix until thickened.

Divide the mixture evenly between the prepared muffin tin, then bake for 15 minutes or until the custard has darkened and the pastry is golden in colour.

Remove from the oven and dust with powdered sugar and ground cinnamon. Serve and enjoy!

9. Lemon Custard Slices

For those that enjoy a dessert with a citrusy flavour, give this a try!

Prep time: 10 minutes

Cook time: 40 minutes

Servings: 8

Ingredients:

- 4 eggs, whites & yolks separated
- ½ cup butter, melted
- ¾ cup sugar
- ¾ cup flour
- 2 lemons, juice & zest
- 1 ¾ cups milk
- powdered sugar for dusting

Directions:

Preheat your oven to 325° Fahrenheit. Grease a casserole dish with butter.

Whisk the egg yolks and sugar in a bowl until well combined. Add the lemon zest and juice, then add the flour, milk and sugar. Mix until all ingredients are well combined.

In a small bowl, whisk the egg whites until peaks have formed. Carefully fold the egg whites into the egg yolk mixture.

Transfer the mixture to the prepared casserole dish and bake for 40 minutes. After baking for 35 minutes, cover with a piece of foil and continue to bake for another 15 minutes. Serve and enjoy!

10. Homemade Vanilla Ice Cream

This a yummy homemade treat that you and your loved ones will surely enjoy!

Prep time: 10 minutes

Cook time: 10 minutes

Servings: 4

Ingredients:

- 1 vanilla pod
- 4 egg yolks (make mousse with whites of eggs)
- 1/3 cup sugar
- 1 ¼ cups milk
- 1 ¼ cups cream

Directions:

Heat the milk and cream in a pan over medium heat. Scrape the vanilla pod seeds from the pod into the pan and add the pod to the pan too. Cook for about 5 minutes.

Mix the sugar and egg yolks in a bowl until light and frothy. Remove the vanilla pod, pour the milk into the egg mixture, and whisk.

Pour the custard mix back into the saucepan and heat over low while stirring for about 5 minutes.

Pour the thick mixture into a container and cool. Add to the ice cream machine and churn as instructed. Place the container in the freezer, remove it every half an hour and stir to help break down ice crystals. Continue to repeat this process for the next 3 hours.

Place the container in the fridge about 15 minutes before you want to serve it to help soften it. Serve and enjoy!

11. Spicy Egg Rolls

It makes for a perfect light and yummy lunchtime meal!

Prep time: 10 minutes

Cook time: 5 minutes

Servings: 2

Ingredients:

- 4 eggs
- 1 tablespoon Chorizo, chopped
- 2 tablespoons milk
- 1 tablespoon cilantro, chopped
- 1 tablespoon sweet chili sauce
- 3 green onions, finely chopped
- 2 tortilla wraps
- 1 teaspoon butter
- 1 teaspoon olive oil

Directions:

Whisk the milk and eggs in a bowl until well combined.

In a small pan, melt your butter over low heat. Add your egg mixture and cook over low heat for a few minutes or until your eggs scramble.

Stir in the cilantro, Chorizo and green onions once lumps appear.

Put the tortilla wraps on the serving plate, then divide the scrambled eggs evenly between them. Drizzle the chili sauce over and roll up the tortillas. Serve and enjoy!

12. Egg Clouds on Toast

This is a wonderful and simple recipe for breakfast or lunchtime!

Prep time: 5 minutes

Cook time: 8 minutes

Servings: 4

Ingredients:

- 4 large eggs
- 4 slices of thick bread of your choice
- ½ cup grated cheese of your choice

Directions:

Begin by preheating your oven to 400° Fahrenheit. Line a baking sheet with parchment paper.

Lightly toast thick bread slices of your choice.

Separate the eggs, keeping the egg yolks whole. Whisk your egg whites in a small bowl until peaks form.

Divide most of your egg whites between four toasted slices. Make a dent in the egg whites and add in the egg yolks there.

Cover with the remaining egg white mixture and sprinkle with grated cheese.

Place in the oven for 8 minutes or until the yolks are cooked to your liking. Serve and enjoy!

13. Lentil Moussaka

Enjoy this healthy meal full of goodness with loved ones!

Prep time: 10 minutes

Cook time: 50 minutes

Servings: 4-6

Ingredients:

- 3 eggs
- 1 tablespoon olive oil
- 2 garlic cloves, crushed
- 1 onion, chopped
- 1 ½ cups red lentils
- 1 (14 ounces) can tomatoes, chopped
- 2 eggplants, sliced into 1-inch pieces
- 1 teaspoon rosemary, dried
- 1 teaspoon thyme, dried
- 1 teaspoon sea salt (fine)
- 1 teaspoon oregano, dried
- 3 cups vegetable broth
- 1 cup cheddar cheese, grated
- 1 tablespoon butter
- 1 tablespoon flour
- 1 cup milk

Directions:

Begin by preheating your oven to 400° Fahrenheit. Grease a casserole dish with butter.

Heat your oil in a pan over medium heat, then add onion and garlic. Cook for a few minutes or until soft.

Add the herbs, salt, lentils, stock and tomatoes. Bring everything to a boil and cover it with a lid. Simmer the mixture for about 20 minutes.

Pour the mixture into the prepared casserole dish and top with eggplant slices.

In a small pan, add the butter, flour and milk over low heat and stir to combine. Cook until a smooth and glossy sauce is created. Whisk in the eggs and cheese, then pour over the top of the eggplants and lentils.

Place the casserole dish into the oven and bake for 30 minutes or until the top is golden and bubbling. Serve with a green salad, and enjoy!

14. Leek, Pea & Spinach Frittata

A dish that I have served for lunch and dinner!

Prep time: 8 minutes

Cook time: 20 minutes

Servings: 4

Ingredients:

- 6 eggs
- 1 tablespoon olive oil
- 1 tablespoon milk
- 3 ounces feta cheese
- 8 ounces fresh spinach shredded
- 2 leeks, shredded
- 1 garlic clove, crushed
- ½ cup potatoes, cooked & thinly sliced
- ½ cup peas, defrosted

Directions:

Heat your oil in a large frying pan over medium heat and add garlic and leeks. Cook through or until the leeks are soft.

Add the spinach, potatoes and peas and stir to combine.

Whisk your eggs with the milk and pour them into the frying pan. Slowly move the eggs around in the pan until they have set on the bottom.

Crumble the feta cheese into the frying pan. Make sure to use an oven-proof pan. Place pan under grill setting in oven for 10-minutes or until the top becomes golden in colour. Serve and enjoy!

15. Prawn & Spinach Omelette

A delightful seafood egg dish makes for a yummy weekend breakfast or lunch meal!

Prep time: 10 minutes

Cook time: 6 minutes

Servings: 1

Ingredients:

- 3 eggs
- 2 cups fresh spinach, finely chopped
- ½ cup cooked prawns
- 1 teaspoon olive oil
- ½ teaspoon sea salt (fine)
- ¼ cup Parmesan, freshly grated

Directions:

Add chopped spinach to a colander, then pour boiled water over it until it is wilted. Drain the excess water from the spinach.

In a frying pan, heat the oil and whisk the eggs and salt together, then pour into the hot pan and swirl around.

Using your spatula keep the eggs moving so they do not set on the bottom.

Sprinkle the Parmesan and prawns onto one side of the omelet and fold over the other half to form a half-circle with prawns inside.

Heat the omelet for about 2 minutes per side. Serve immediately with a nice crisp green salad of your choice and enjoy!

16. Breakfast Egg Mushrooms

This is an excellent dish for mushroom and egg lovers!

Prep time: 8 minutes

Cook time: 10 minutes

Servings: 1

Ingredients:

- 1 tablespoon of sunflower seeds
- 2 eggs
- 2 large Portobello mushrooms
- 1 tablespoon sour cream

Directions:

Preheat your oven to 400° Fahrenheit. Line a baking sheet with parchment paper.

Clean the mushrooms and remove the stalks. Place the mushrooms upside down on the prepared baking sheet.

Crack the eggs into the mushroom caps. Add half a tablespoon of sour cream to each egg and sprinkle top with sunflower seeds.

Bake for about 10 minutes or until the eggs are set to your liking. Serve and enjoy!

17. Breakfast Casserole

An excellent casserole breakfast dish to serve for a weekend breakfast treat!

Prep time: 10 minutes

Cook time: 55 minutes

Servings: 6

Ingredients:

- 6 eggs
- 1 lb. Bacon, chopped
- 1 large potato, peeled & grated
- 1 tablespoon olive oil
- 1 cup grated cheese of your choosing
- 1 onion, finely chopped
- 1 ½ cups cottage cheese
- 1 tablespoon fresh parsley, chopped

Directions:

Begin by preheating your oven to 400° Fahrenheit. Lightly grease the casserole dish with butter or oil.

Heat oil in a large frying pan over medium heat. Next, add in the bacon and onions and cook for about 8 minutes or until cooked through. Add the potato to the pan and continue to cook for about 5 minutes over high heat or until the potato is soft.

In a mixing bowl, whisk the eggs and cheese together.

Remove the bacon, onions and potato from the heat and allow to cool.

Combine the egg mixture with the cooled potato mixture in the prepared casserole dish. Sprinkle top with parsley and extra cheese.

Bake the casserole in the oven for about 45 minutes or until the casserole is golden in colour. Serve immediately and enjoy!

18. Smoked Cod Kedgeree

A savoury and healthy meal to provide for your family and loved ones!

Prep time: 8 minutes

Cook time: 15 minutes

Servings: 4

Ingredients:

- 4 eggs, soft-boiled & peeled
- 12 ounces Smoked cod fillet
- 6 peppercorns
- 1 cup milk
- 2 bay leafs
- 1 onion, finely diced
- 1 cup Basmati rice
- 1 teaspoon ground coriander
- 1 teaspoon ground turmeric
- 2 teaspoons curry powder
- 1 tablespoon parsley, chopped
- 1 tablespoon chives, chopped
- 2 teaspoons olive oil

Directions:

Poach your cod in the milk with peppercorns and bay leafs. Simmer for about 10 minutes.

In a saucepan, heat the oil and cook the onion over medium heat, adding in all the spices for about 2 minutes.

Add in the rice and stir to combine the mixture. Add in 2 cups of water to mix and simmer for an additional 12 minutes with the lid on the pan.

Flake the cod into large pieces and add to the saucepan. Slice the eggs into quarters and add them to the saucepan and stir. Serve immediately and enjoy!

19. Spaghetti Carbonara

The perfect light and flavourful dish to serve on a hot summer day!

Prep time: 10 minutes

Cook time: 15 minutes

Servings: 4

Ingredients:

- 2 eggs
- 8 ounces spaghetti
- 1 teaspoon olive oil
- 1 tablespoon cream
- 6 slices bacon, chopped
- 1 cup Parmesan, freshly grated
- 2 garlic cloves, crushed
- 1 tablespoon of freshly chopped herbs such as chives and parsley

Directions:

Heat water to boiling in a large saucepan, add the spaghetti and cook according to packet instructions.

Heat a frying pan with your olive oil over medium heat. Add the bacon and cook until the bacon is crispy. Drain the oil.

Whisk your eggs, garlic and cream in a mixing bowl.

Drain your spaghetti and reserve ½ cup of the cooking water. Combine the egg mixture with spaghetti. Add your Parmesan cheese and stir to combine. Reserve extra Parmesan for serving.

Add to serving plates and sprinkle top with chopped herbs and extra Parmesan. Serve and enjoy!

20. Smoked Salmon & Chive Quiche

Enjoy this healthy meal, perhaps when you are enjoying a sunny day!

Prep time: 10 minutes

Cook time: 45 minutes

Servings: 6

Ingredients:

- 4 eggs
- 6 ounces smoked salmon trimmings
- 1 cup milk
- 3 tablespoons fresh chives, chopped
- 2 tablespoons cream cheese
- 1 tablespoon fresh parsley, chopped
- 7 ounces flour
- 3 ounces butter, cubed
- 1 teaspoon sea salt (fine)

Directions:

Begin by heating your oven to 400° Fahrenheit. Grease a 9" deep flan dish with butter or oil.

To prepare the pastry, rub the flour, butter and salt with some iced cold water. Create a smooth dough using your hands and a rolling pin. Leave your dough to rest for about half an hour.

Roll out your pastry on a floured board then line the flan dish with the pastry. Bake the pastry shell for 10 minutes or until cooked.

Whisk your milk, eggs, herbs and cream cheese together.

Scatter your salmon trimmings over the bottom of the pastry, then pour the egg mixture over the salmon trimmings.

Bake in the oven for 30 minutes or until the eggs are set and the top is golden.

Remove the dish from the oven, then place on the counter to cool at room temperature. Serve with a green salad of your choice and top with extra fresh chopped chives. Serve and enjoy!

21. Sausage & Egg Pie

A great meal to serve for a yummy weekend breakfast meal!

Prep time: 10 minutes

Cook time: 45 minutes

Servings: 4

Ingredients:

- 4 eggs, hard-boiled & peeled
- ½ cup breadcrumbs
- 3 cups sausage meat
- 1 teaspoon Marjoram, dried
- 1 teaspoon thyme, dried
- 1 extra egg (beaten to make an egg wash)
- 1 large sheet of puff pastry, cut in half

Directions:

Begin by preheating your oven to 400° Fahrenheit—grease the baking sheet with butter or oil.

Lay out your puff pastry, mix sausage meat with herbs, and divide it into two portions.

Roll one portion of meat into a long log and place it on one piece of puff pastry in the middle. Flatten the log down to prepare a bed to line the hard-boiled eggs on.

Brush the meat with egg wash and cover with another piece of pastry to encase the eggs. Seal the pastry around the edges, removing any excess pastry. Add egg wash over the whole pastry.

Place into the oven and bake for about 45 minutes or until the pastry is golden in colour. Serve this dish hot or cold! Serve and enjoy!

22. Chickpea Shakshuka

An excellent dish to serve to your lunch quests!

Prep time: 8 minutes

Cook time: 30 minutes

Servings: 4

Ingredients:

- 4 eggs
- 1 teaspoon olive oil
- 1 onion, finely chopped
- 2 garlic cloves, crushed
- 2 cups chickpeas
- 1 teaspoon sweet smoked paprika
- 1 teaspoon sea salt (fine)
- 1 teaspoon mild chili powder
- 1 teaspoon ground cumin
- 2 (14 ounces) cans of tomatoes, chopped
- small bunch of coriander, chopped

Directions:

Begin by preheating your oven to 400° Fahrenheit. Grease a casserole dish with butter or oil.

In a pan, heat your oil over medium heat. Add your onion and garlic to the pan and cook for a few minutes or until soft.

Add the cumin, paprika and chili powder to the pan and stir to combine.

Stir in the chickpeas and tomatoes to pan and continue to cook for another 15 minutes or until the mixture thickens.

Add the mixture to the prepared casserole dish and make four dents in it. Crack the eggs into the dents.

Place the casserole dish in the prepared oven and bake for about 12 minutes or until the eggs are cooked to your liking. Sprinkle the top with fresh chopped herbs. Serve and enjoy!

23. Toad-In-A-Hole

The perfect dish to serve to those that enjoy a good hearty breakfast!

Prep time: 10 minutes

Cook time: 45 minutes

Servings: 4

Ingredients:

- 4 eggs
- 4 large sausages
- 8 pieces of bacon
- 1 cup milk
- 1 cup flour
- 1 tablespoon olive oil
- 1 tablespoon butter
- 1 teaspoon sea salt (fine)

Directions:

Begin by preheating your oven to 400° Fahrenheit. Grease the casserole dish with butter or oil.

In a mixing bowl, whisk your milk, flour and eggs until smooth. Let the batter rest for about half an hour.

Place the prepared casserole dish in the oven for about 1 minute or until it becomes hot. Wrap the bacon pieces around the sausages. Add to the hot prepared casserole dish. Turn sausages over to coat with oil.

Pour the egg mixture over the sausages, place the casserole dish back into the oven, and bake for 40 minutes or until golden in colour. Serve and enjoy!

24. Egg Wraps

This easy-to-prepare dish makes for an excellent on-the-go breakfast or lunch meal!

Prep time: 8 minutes

Cook time: 8 minutes

Servings: 4

Ingredients:

- 4 eggs
- 1 cup grated cheese of your choice
- 4 tortilla wraps
- 4 slices ham
- BBQ sauce as needed

Directions:

Take four pieces of foil and lay each wrap on a piece of foil.

Add a piece of ham to the wrap in the middle. Make a circle from grated cheese around the ham pieces. Crack an egg into each circle, then add a bit of BBQ sauce to the eggs.

Fold the wraps on opposite sides until you have created a square and secure it with foil.

Add to the baking tray and place in the oven for about 10 minutes or until the eggs are cooked through. Serve and enjoy!

25. Amazing Waffle Breakfast

A personal favourite breakfast meal of mine that is yummy and quick to prepare!

Prep time: 10 minutes

Cook time: 30 minutes

Servings: 4

Ingredients:

- 6 eggs
- 6 waffles
- 4 tablespoons light brown sugar
- ½ teaspoon ground cinnamon
- 4 tablespoons milk
- 1 tablespoon flaked almond

Directions:

Begin by preheating your oven to 400° Fahrenheit. Grease a small casserole dish with some butter or oil.

In a mixing bowl, combine milk, eggs and cinnamon by whisking until well combined.

Place your waffles into the prepared casserole dish and pour the egg mixture over the waffles. Sprinkle the top with flaked almonds and sugar over the top. Leave the waffles to soak at room temperature for 30 minutes.

Put your casserole dish into the prepared oven and bake for 30 minutes or until golden in colour. Serve and enjoy!

26. Over Easy Croissants

A lovely and light dish to serve, along with a cup of coffee or tea!

Prep time: 8 minutes

Cook time: 10 minutes

Servings: 1

Ingredients:

- 1 egg
- 1 croissant
- 2 tablespoons grated cheese (of your choice)
- 1 slice of cooked ham

Directions:

Begin by preheating your oven to 400° Fahrenheit. Line a baking pan with a sheet of parchment paper.

Slice open your croissant. Put the slice of ham into the bottom of the sliced croissant.

Heat your egg in a small pan over medium heat until almost cooked to your preference.

Set the fried egg on top of the ham in the croissant, sprinkle with grated cheese, and cover by closing the croissant.

Bake in the prepared oven for 5 minutes or until the cheese is melted. Serve and enjoy!

27. Chocolate Dotted Bread & Butter Pudding

A great tasting and yummy dish that will please those dining at your table!

Prep time: 12 minutes

Cook time: 45 minutes

Servings: 6

Ingredients:

- 4 eggs
- 8 slices of thick bread, crusts removed
- 3 tablespoons of light brown sugar plus 1 tablespoon for sprinkling on top
- ½ cup chocolate chips
- ½ cup chocolate spread
- 1 ½ cups milk

Directions:

Begin by preheating your oven to 400° Fahrenheit. Grease a casserole dish with butter or oil.

Spread the chocolate spread onto the slices of bread and cut them into triangle shapes. Place them into the casserole dish, and scatter chocolate chips between the slices.

Whisk the milk, sugar and eggs in a mixing bowl until well combined. Pour the mixture over the bread.

Leave the bread to soak for about one hour, then sprinkle the remaining sugar over the top.

Bake in the prepared oven for 45 minutes or until golden in colour. Remove and serve this comforting custard-like dish and enjoy!

28. Chocolate Mousse

A light and delightful treat sure to be a popular choice with chocolate lovers!

Prep time: 5 minutes

Cook time: 5 minutes

Servings: 4

Ingredients:

- 2 tablespoons sugar
- 4 ounces dark chocolate, cut into pieces
- 4 eggs whites

Directions:

Whisk your egg whites to form stiff peaks in a large bowl. Gradually add the sugar.

Heat a small pan of water over medium heat and heat the chocolate over it for about 5 minutes or until it has melted.

Add the chocolate to the egg mixture and mix carefully.

Divide the mousse between four serving dishes or ramekins—place in the fridge for about 2-hours. Serve and enjoy!

29. Custard Tart

Enjoy these citrus-flavoured tarts, perhaps served with coffee and tea!

Prep time: 5 minutes

Cook time: 45 minutes

Servings: 10

Ingredients:

- 6 eggs
- 2 egg yolks
- 1 teaspoon nutmeg
- 1/3 cup light brown sugar
- 2 teaspoons vanilla extract
- ¼ cup milk
- 1 cup cream
- 1 baked sweet pastry case (about 9-inches)

Directions:

Begin by preheating your oven to 325° Fahrenheit.

Whisk your cream, milk, eggs, sugar and vanilla in a mixing bowl. Add mixture to saucepan over medium heat for about 5 minutes.

Pour the mixture through a sieve into a pastry case. Sprinkle top with nutmeg and bake for 45 minutes or until custard is set.

Remove from the oven and let cool at room temperature for 10 minutes. Serve and enjoy!

30. Breakfast Tart

A lovely and easy-to-prepare breakfast dish that you are sure to love!

Prep time: 5 minutes

Cook time: 25 minutes

Servings: 4

Ingredients:

- 4 eggs
- 1 sheet of puff pastry
- 1 tablespoon Worcestershire sauce
- 4 tablespoons tomatoes, finely chopped
- 12 cocktail sausages
- 4 slices cooked ham

Directions:

Prepare your oven by setting it to 400° Fahrenheit. Line a baking tray with parchment paper.

Slice the pastry into four large squares. Add 1 tablespoon of tomatoes for each pastry square.

Place four sausages around the outside of the tomato sauce. Set on top a piece of ham on each pastry and push a little in the middle of them to form a dent.

Bake in the oven for about 15 minutes, then remove from the oven. Crack an egg into each dent in the ham slices and return to the oven. Continue to bake until the pastry is crispy and has risen on all sides. Serve and enjoy!

Conclusion

I want to offer my gratitude to you for supporting my cookbook. I truly hope you and your loved ones will enjoy and use this collection of egg-based recipes as much as I have and still do! We are all seeking things in life that will help improve our overall health and well-being! One way to find those aides is to add healthy food choices to your daily diet! All of these recipes have one thing in common: they all include eggs in their ingredients! Adding eggs to your diet will be a step towards improving your overall health. Another incredible plus about these recipes is that they are not complicated but easy to prepare! I wish you many happy years of preparing and sharing these yummy egg-based dishes!

Thank You

THANK YOU

The gratitude I feel for your purchase of my book cannot be expressed in words. Each sale shows me that individuals are benefiting from my experiences and knowledge. Becoming a writer was a decision I made because it allows me to share my skills and expertise with others.

Out of the numerous books available, you chose mine, which is extremely special to me. I have no doubt that the information presented in the book will be useful and informative for you.

Please remember to leave feedback once you've finished reading the book. Every piece of feedback, no matter how small, is invaluable to me in creating even better books. I listen carefully to my readers and take their suggestions into account when developing new content. Your honest feedback will be incorporated into my next books.

Thank you once again for your support.

Alain Duke

Printed in Great Britain
by Amazon